Letters to the Forgotten
Your Struggles Do Not Define You

Letters to the Forgotten
Your Struggles Do Not Define You

Letters to the Forgotten
Your Struggles Do Not Define You

**Letters to the Forgotten:
Your Struggles Do Not Define You**

Letters to the Forgotten
Your Struggles Do Not Define You

Letters to the Forgotten
Your Struggles Do Not Define You

Letters to the Forgotten:
Your Struggles Do Not Define You
~ Lena Ma

© *2020*

Letters to the Forgotten
Your Struggles Do Not Define You

Letters to the Forgotten
Your Struggles Do Not Define You

Letters to the Forgotten
Your Struggles Do Not Define You

TABLE OF CONTENTS

Prologue

14

Chapter One

A Letter To Those Overwhelmed By Anxiety:
We Are All Warriors

20

Chapter Two

A Letter To Those Feeling Lost And Alone:
You Matter, And You Will Be Found

26

Chapter Three

A Letter To Those Fighting A Battle Within:
You Are Stronger Than You Think

32

Letters to the Forgotten
Your Struggles Do Not Define You

Chapter Four
A Letter To Those Dealing With Toxic People:
It's Okay To Leave;
You Do Not Owe Them Your Life

38

Chapter Five
A Letter To Those Dealing With A Broken Heart:
You Deserve Better

44

Chapter Six
A Letter To Those Who Feel Like Their Life Is Falling Apart:
It Is, But You Don't Have To

50

Chapter Seven
A Letter To Those Struggling With Acceptance:
Begin By Learning To Accept Yourself

56

Chapter Eight
A Letter To Those Feeling Pressured To Succeed:
Societal Standards Are Only Optional;
You Can Create Your Own Rules

62

Letters to the Forgotten
Your Struggles Do Not Define You

Chapter Nine
A Letter To Those Overwhelmed With Stress And Frustration:
Breathe
68

Chapter Ten
A Letter To Those Searching For Self-Love:
You Already Have It
74

Letter To Me
A Letter To Those Fighting To Survive:
Live, So Others Can Also Live
84

Letter To Me
A Letter To Those Who Struggle To Forgive Themselves:
Seek Forgiveness From Those Who Believe You Deserve Forgiveness
86

Letter To Me
A Letter To Those Who Have Been Rejected:
Those Who Rejected You Only Deprived Themselves
88

Letters to the Forgotten
Your Struggles Do Not Define You

Letter To Me
A Letter To Those Who Do Not Believe In Themselves:
Live For Today, And Eventually You Will
90

Letter To Me
A Letter To Those Who Find It Difficult To Speak Up:
Be The Courageous Ones Who Stand Up For Those Who Cannot
92

Letter To Me
A Letter To Those Who Need A Supportive Hand:
I Am Here, And I Am Not Going Anywhere
94

Epilogue
96

Letters to the Forgotten
Your Struggles Do Not Define You

Letters to the Forgotten
Your Struggles Do Not Define You

Letters to the Forgotten
Your Struggles Do Not Define You

PROLOGUE

We all know the saying, "Never judge a book by its cover." Sadly, few of us follow this mantra, and we judge everyone and everything without an attempt to know and understand them. We have all been victims and perpetrators of hate, criticism, and ugliness.

We have all opened our mouths seconds too soon and have forgotten that we are human, just like everyone else, struggling to survive in this world.
Life is difficult enough without the

Letters to the Forgotten
Your Struggles Do Not Define You

harsh words of our peers.

We fight instead of love.
We push away instead of understand.
We falsely believe that we are superior to others because of our looks, our status, our upbringings, or just our grandiose mentalities.

We often forget how, without the help of those we criticize, our society would not stand the way it does today, even if it is not apparent at the time.

We forget that, as much as we push people away, it is the same people we push away that want to understand us the most.
But we are scared.
We are scared to lose the mask we so meticulously crafted for ourselves.

We are scared to become vulnerable because we have been hurt before.
We are scared to trust anyone but ourselves because we believe they will never understand us.
We all believe we are unique, with our own unique problems and struggles, and sharing these problems will cause everyone to despise us and look down on us.

Our problems are not unique, nor are they so different and farfetched from everyone else's that we need to shelter them from the world.

Letters to the Forgotten
Your Struggles Do Not Define You

Let's not forget that we are all the same.
We are all part of one family who struggle to fit in, and we just want to be loved.
We are all beautiful human beings despite the many actions and/or words we express to prove to ourselves and others otherwise.

We are not beautiful based on the standard norms of beauty.
Beauty comes from our hearts.
If we feel beautiful, then we are, despite hateful words of others.
Never let anyone else tell you or make you feel ugly and worthless because you create your own beauty.

These letters were written from my heart to yours because we all need to be reminded that we are all special, even when life tells us that we are not.

These letters serve as constant reminders for all of us to love and accept ourselves, even during times when no one else does.

Letters to the Forgotten
Your Struggles Do Not Define You

Letters to the Forgotten
Your Struggles Do Not Define You

LETTERS TO YOU

Letters to the Forgotten
Your Struggles Do Not Define You

Letters to the Forgotten
Your Struggles Do Not Define You

CHAPTER ONE

**A Letter To Those Overwhelmed By Anxiety:
We Are All Warriors**

Imagine getting on a plane and completely forgetting
whether you turned your stove off.
How do you feel?
Now imagine experiencing that feeling every minute of every day.
That is what anxiety feels like.

Letters to the Forgotten
Your Struggles Do Not Define You

Anxiety is being in a state of constant worry and not being able to turn it off.
But anxiety is not a disorder.
Anxiety is not a flaw.
Anxiety is a survival technique and protection mechanism designed to help you get through life.

While everyone else is blindly jumping into the hole, you are processing what is in that hole, and the consequences you will face if you also jump.
Anxiety is a creative process inside your head that helps you sort through to the best plan of action before diving in head first.

Anxiety is not a fault you should hide.
Instead, it is a strength you should embrace because it helps make you stronger and more courageous to face the monsters in this world.

People will tell you that it is crippling to live with constant worry inside your head because you never get the chance to relax.
But you do relax.
You are smart enough to know that once you figure out the best plan of action, you can sit back in peace, knowing that you have made the right decision.

Anxiety does not make you flawed.
Anxiety makes you a warrior because you are able to turn clutter into blueprints in order to survive.

Letters to the Forgotten
Your Struggles Do Not Define You

Being on your toes all the time helps you get through life in one piece.
There are days where you may want to give up, days where you may want to just make an impulsive decision and move on, worry-free.
I get it.
Being worried all the time is time-consuming, and it is extremely difficult when you feel like everyone else is moving forward except you.
But the truth is, they are not moving forward.

We are all moving at our own pace, and those who seem to be moving forward, can also move back.
No one knows the exact path that they are going to take.
This is just your path, and that is okay.
Accept that you are living a creative process and love yourself for that.
It is an amazing place to be because you are turning fire into flame, and that is a skill to be proud of.

Letters to the Forgotten
Your Struggles Do Not Define You

Write down all the words that are running
Through your head this very moment.
Do not think.
Just write.

Letters to the Forgotten
Your Struggles Do Not Define You

*Draw an image that represents how
you are feeling this very moment.
Do not think.
Just draw.*

Letters to the Forgotten
Your Struggles Do Not Define You

Letters to the Forgotten
Your Struggles Do Not Define You

CHAPTER TWO

**A Letter To Those Feeling Lost And Alone:
You Matter, And You Will Be Found**

Do you feel lost?
Do you feel like the world around you is moving on while you remain stagnant and stuck?
Do you feel as if no one will notice if you suddenly disappeared into the darkness?
You feel alone.

Letters to the Forgotten
Your Struggles Do Not Define You

You feel unaccomplished.
You feel invisible and simply trudging through life, one monotonous step at a time.
But this is just a feeling.

Everyone, even the most "successful", at one time, has also experienced this feeling.
Remember, feelings are not reality, and "feeling lost" is not "being lost".

You are present, you are here, and you matter in this world.
You may not think that people around you see you, but they do.
If you are gone, they will notice an absence.

You feel that they do not notice you now because they know that you are always there, that you are reliable and loyal.
This feeling will fade.
Although it seems never-ending, someone will come along and find you again.
It may be another person or it may be you.

Someone will help you find light again and show you how this world, and the lives of people around you, will completely change if you are gone.
You don't have to feel like you have purpose now because you are purpose.

Being alive means you are already found.
You may not notice, but people see you.

Letters to the Forgotten
Your Struggles Do Not Define You

When you look in the mirror, you see you.
That's all the evidence that you need.
So just keep breathing.

Stop trying so hard to be seen because your presence is already radiant.
Accept that you are simply experiencing a feeling, and that reality is much more different.

More importantly, if you are ever feeling alone, remember that someone else in this world is also feeling the same.
And if you can find a reason to feel hope again, maybe they can too.

Be the change for yourself and for others.

Letters to the Forgotten
Your Struggles Do Not Define You

Write down all the words that are running
Through your head this very moment.
Do not think.
Just write.

Letters to the Forgotten
Your Struggles Do Not Define You

*Draw an image that represents how
you are feeling this very moment.
Do not think.
Just draw.*

Letters to the Forgotten
Your Struggles Do Not Define You

CHAPTER THREE

**A Letter To Those Fighting A Battle Within:
You Are Stronger Than You Think**

The greatest battle we will ever fight is the battle within ourselves. The greatest enemy we will ever have is our own conscience. The greatest compassion we will ever feel is our own self-acceptance.

Every day, we are in a constant battle with ourselves, whether it involves how we look, how we behave, words that do or do not

Letters to the Forgotten
Your Struggles Do Not Define You

come out of our mouths, how we love, who we love, what we become, who we become, etc.

Our heads become convoluted with back and forth nonsense about how we are not good enough.
Isn't it enough that we already fight the hate and judgments of others?
Why make life that much more difficult by adding onto the war?

We are the most intelligent yet the most vulnerable.
We know who we are and who we want to be but doubt ourselves every step of the way.

We constantly compare ourselves to others in how we are not pretty enough, not smart enough, not rich enough, or not successful enough, and in return, we completely ignore the gifts that we do have.
We are pretty enough.
We are smart enough.
We are rich enough, and we are successful enough.
What we are not, however, is confident enough.

Even if we try to tell ourselves every day that we are good and worthy, we still let the influences of others change our minds.
But let's give self-doubt, external hate, and internal battles the finger, and walk away with pride, proud of who we already are and confident enough to stand by ourselves when no one else will.

Letters to the Forgotten
Your Struggles Do Not Define You

We may be our greatest enemies, but we are also our greatest allies, and by learning to stop fighting our internal battles and accepting parts of us we believe are flaws, we are relieved from our worst heartaches.
Every one of us is born different.

When we try to be like everyone else, we lose the qualities that make us unique and different.
When we try so hard to fit in, we become lost, and we lose our individualities.
Our doubt and self-hatred are strong, polluted by the society around us.
I get it.

However, I also believe that we all have the strength to overcome anything, and the moment we can conquer our sins against ourselves, that is the moment we can declare victory against life's war.

Letters to the Forgotten
Your Struggles Do Not Define You

Write down all the words that are running
Through your head this very moment.
Do not think.
Just write.

Letters to the Forgotten
Your Struggles Do Not Define You

Draw an image that represents how
you are feeling this very moment.
Do not think.
Just draw.

Letters to the Forgotten
Your Struggles Do Not Define You

CHAPTER FOUR

**A Letter To Those Dealing With Toxic People:
It's Okay To Leave;
You Do Not Owe Them Your Life**

We all have those people in our lives, the ones who only contribute stress, negativity, and misery without the benefit of anything positive.
These people can be our families, our friends, our partners, or our colleagues.
These are the people who know we care and take advantage of us.

Letters to the Forgotten
Your Struggles Do Not Define You

These are the people who will screw us over every chance they get because they know we will always be there.
These are the charmers, the ones with the face of an angel but the heart of the devil.
These are the people we need to walk away from.

I recently lost a friend who would constantly cut me out of his life for simply having an opinion and not catering to his every need.
I recently lost a partner who, no matter what I did, would always leave, knowing I would take him back whenever he saw convenient.

Losing someone is never easy, despite how terribly they behaved.
We invest so much time and energy into people that we feel guilty if we leave and betrayed if they leave.

But what happens when we stay?
What happens when we let toxic people walk all over us, forgiving them unconditionally while all they do is bring us pain?
We end up losing our own lives and our own happiness to protect that of others.

It is time we finally put our feet down and walk away from those who only bring us heartache.
It is time we stop feeling guilty for living for our own happiness.
We can still love toxic people, but we also need to learn when to walk away before we completely lose our voice and our freedom.

Letters to the Forgotten
Your Struggles Do Not Define You

We need to stand up against those who treat us poorly,
and more times than not, walking away from
them is the best way to do so.
Don't ever feel guilty for taking back your own life, especially
when the other person doesn't feel guilty for stealing it.

When you start surrounding yourself with positive people who
only want the best for you, you start realizing that you have
choices and a mind of your own.
Unconditionally loving someone who doesn't love you back only
shows that you have a heart that should be shared with those who
will also share their hearts with you.

Do not regret having shared your life with a toxic person.
Loving someone who hurt you is a beautiful gift and an incredible
feat of selflessness.

Letters to the Forgotten
Your Struggles Do Not Define You

Write down all the words that are running
Through your head this very moment.
Do not think.
Just write.

Letters to the Forgotten
Your Struggles Do Not Define You

Draw an image that represents how
you are feeling this very moment.
Do not think.
Just draw.

Letters to the Forgotten
Your Struggles Do Not Define You

CHAPTER FIVE

**A Letter To Those Dealing With A Broken Heart:
You Deserve Better**

We have all been there.
A broken heart, crushed by someone we once loved and trusted.
Whether it is a short-term breakup or a long-term divorce,
a broken heart is a broken heart, and it leaves us feeling like we
just want to die.

But it will get better, I promise!

Letters to the Forgotten
Your Struggles Do Not Define You

It may not feel like it in the moment, but think of all the other times you have dealt with the same feeling, and with time, the pain has lessened, right?

I know you're thinking that this time isn't the same as the other times, or this person meant so much more than the ones in the past.
I know the feeling.
I have been there, and trust me, things were not pretty for me either.

Even if you do not believe that it will get better, believe that you deserve to be loved and cared for by someone who doesn't walk out on you or betray you when life becomes difficult.
Believe that one day, someone will come along and give you the world rather than vice versa.
Believe that you will find someone, where no matter what you say or do, that person will still love you regardless because they see and love you as a person, not for your actions or status.

Believe that, even though you may never forget the current person, you will replace this face with a new one.
Believe that you are worth so much more than the betrayals of someone who hurt you.
So often we still settle for people who may not be the best for us.

We see arguments and unfaithfulness as a commonality rather than a problem, and we ignore our brains telling us that there is

Letters to the Forgotten
Your Struggles Do Not Define You

someone better out there because we are so afraid of ending up alone.

We settle for relationships where the other person does not love us, but instead only tolerates us enough to stick around, because we lie to ourselves that this is the best we can do.
But you know it isn't!
Even if you may not see it, I see it!

I see that we are all beautiful and kind-hearted people who deserve to be treated with the same love and compassion we give others.
We deserve so much more than someone who can only love us conditionally.
I promise that the right person will come around.
Patience and self-respect are keys to all happiness.

The more love we show ourselves, the more love others can begin to show us.
The radiance that comes from within us captures the radiance that we crave from those around us.

Letters to the Forgotten
Your Struggles Do Not Define You

Write down all the words that are running
Through your head this very moment.
Do not think.
Just write.

Letters to the Forgotten
Your Struggles Do Not Define You

*Draw an image that represents how
you are feeling this very moment.
Do not think.
Just draw.*

Letters to the Forgotten
Your Struggles Do Not Define You

CHAPTER SIX

**A Letter To Those Who Feel Like Their Life Is Falling Apart:
It Is, But You Don't Have To**

Everything and everyone around you are either falling apart or destroying themselves.
I get it.
Every minute of the day, you feel like you want to close your eyes for the final time.
Every agony you face, you feel like you would rather die.
I get it.

Letters to the Forgotten
Your Struggles Do Not Define You

Your life is slowly crumbling into pieces, and you are tired of trying to hold it together, just to watch it fall apart again.

Some days you walk past a bridge and wonder, even for a second, how all your problems can finally be over if you just jumped.
I get it.
But I need to tell you that running away or shutting yourself out to avoid situations in which you cannot fix is not the answer.

As painstakingly debilitating as having to deal with problems is, it only helps build you stronger.
Just because moments around you are hell, does not mean you also have to live in hell.

Life will always suck, and you will always feel like you want to end it all rather than face it.
If not this one, it will be the next.
You will even face moments that will rip your soul out and make you wish you were never born.

But when that moment comes, you will be ready.
For you have already claimed victory over your other battles in life.
You will be strong enough to win the war because you have not given up.

Are you still with me?
Good.

Letters to the Forgotten
Your Struggles Do Not Define You

During this next minute, don't do anything else besides read what is on this page.
You have come too far to give up now.
You have fought and won many battles already.
If you stop now, all your achievements would have been for nothing.

You are strong enough to get through whatever it is you are facing because you have done it many times before.

You believe you are not strong enough now, but you are just scared.
I am also terrified.
But where there is fear, there is also courage.
I need you to keep living.
If you can't do it for yourself, do it for me.

I need you to keep fighting so I can also keep fighting.
Let us both come down from the ledge and defeat life together, okay?
I will always be here with you.

Here, take my hand.
Let's go.

Letters to the Forgotten
Your Struggles Do Not Define You

Write down all the words that are running
Through your head this very moment.
Do not think.
Just write.

Letters to the Forgotten
Your Struggles Do Not Define You

Draw an image that represents how
you are feeling this very moment.
Do not think.
Just draw.

Letters to the Forgotten
Your Struggles Do Not Define You

CHAPTER SEVEN

**A Letter To Those Struggling With Acceptance:
Begin By Learning To Accept Yourself**

You crave acceptance.
We all do.
You change your hair, your clothes, even your personality, in attempts to gain acceptance.

You want those around you, peers and strangers alike, to simply like you and accept you for who you already are.

Letters to the Forgotten
Your Struggles Do Not Define You

But they do not.
And it drives you insane.

You continue changing.
You spend hours researching the most likeable personality traits you can possess, and you spend your life-savings on transient lifestyles that you believe will give you an edge, despite your feelings toward them.

You keep trying.
Trying until your body gives out and your brain overloads.
You give until you have nothing left to give except for blood and bones.

Nothing changes.
They still do not accept you.
You still feel like you are on the outside.
No matter what you do, they will never let you in.

You cry.
You want this to end.
You want to stop feeling like you have nothing left.
You just want acceptance.

But you cannot obtain it the one way you have been trying.
So, what do you do?
You try again.
In a different way.
Rather than looking toward your surroundings, you look within.

Letters to the Forgotten
Your Struggles Do Not Define You

Rather than seeking acceptance from your peers and strangers, you seek acceptance from yourself.

You cannot control whether others accept or reject you.
But you can control whether you accept or reject yourself.
Right now, you have been rejecting yourself.
Seeking fulfillment from others because that is what you have been taught to do.

Place your hand over the left side of your chest.
Do you feel that?
Do you feel that rhythmic beating?
That is the melody to your unique life.
From the loving and accepting heart that you possess.

Feel your heart.
Use it.
Remind yourself that you also possess a heart capable of acceptance.
When others fail to see the beauty that you are, place your hand over your chest and remember that you can see your own beauty.

When you crave acceptance from others, remind yourself that you do not have to destroy yourself for it.
You can give acceptance to yourself, and that is all that you need.

Letters to the Forgotten
Your Struggles Do Not Define You

Write down all the words that are running
Through your head this very moment.
Do not think.
Just write.

Letters to the Forgotten
Your Struggles Do Not Define You

Draw an image that represents how
you are feeling this very moment.
Do not think.
Just draw.

Letters to the Forgotten
Your Struggles Do Not Define You

CHAPTER EIGHT

**A Letter To Those Feeling Pressured To Succeed:
Societal Standards Are Only Optional;
You Can Create Your Own Rules**

From the day you were born, what were you told?
Attend the top universities, climb the career ladder, and settle down with a loving family.
You listen with a smile because you have not learned any other way.

Letters to the Forgotten
Your Struggles Do Not Define You

A decade down the road, you realize that life is not the fairytale story you were told as a child.
Life is much more difficult and complicated.

Life gives you the ingredients and options to live that fairytale story, but life also gives you unexpected results.
You continue your journey toward what you were told: education, career, and family.
But that smile is no longer there.

You feel empty.
You tell yourself that you are the only one not succeeding, while everyone else is.

You begin to wonder whether there is something wrong with you, why you are not able to match up to your peers.
Are they simply better at living life?
You look down in despair, unable to pull your head out of your own personal misery.

But then you feel the wind.
You look up.
You look around.
You see everyone robotically moving in the same direction that you were told.
But none of them are smiling.
Even when they are surrounded by diplomas and paychecks.

You question yourself again.

Letters to the Forgotten
Your Struggles Do Not Define You

Why is no one smiling if they are living life the way they should be?

Maybe I am not alone.
Maybe no one has this figured out.
Maybe reality is not a fairytale after all.

If everyone around me is living life the way they were told and are still not happy, maybe happiness comes from living outside the boundaries.

Maybe I can create my own happiness by living the life I choose rather than the life chosen for me.
Maybe I can finally break out of what society has ingrained into my brain and change the way that life should be lived.
Maybe I can learn to smile again.
Just maybe.

Letters to the Forgotten
Your Struggles Do Not Define You

Write down all the words that are running
Through your head this very moment.
Do not think.
Just write.

Letters to the Forgotten
Your Struggles Do Not Define You

*Draw an image that represents how
you are feeling this very moment.
Do not think.
Just draw.*

Letters to the Forgotten
Your Struggles Do Not Define You

CHAPTER NINE

A Letter To Those Overwhelmed With Stress And Frustration: Breathe

I know you have those moments.
Moments where the entire world just seems to aggravate you.
Moments where you wish you could punch a hole through a wall and unleash all the anger you have pent up inside of you.
Moments where you simply want to be isolated and alone, forever.

Letters to the Forgotten
Your Struggles Do Not Define You

Those moments are real.
We have all struggled with those moments.
The moments where we have not been triggered, but the frustration is still there.

You want it to stop.
You hate lashing out at anyone who tries to speak to you because it is not fair to them.
They have done nothing wrong.
Yet, you still unleash.

You feel as if your head is about to explode.
You want it to all go away.
You try distractions.
You try self-medicating.
You even try isolation.
But nothing seems to work.

You just want to stop thinking.
I know.
Just breathe.
Breathe in.
And out.
In.

And out.
In.
Out.
Breathe.

Letters to the Forgotten
Your Struggles Do Not Define You

Breathe.
Breathe.

Letters to the Forgotten
Your Struggles Do Not Define You

Write down all the words that are running
Through your head this very moment.
Do not think.
Just write.

Letters to the Forgotten
Your Struggles Do Not Define You

*Draw an image that represents how
you are feeling this very moment.
Do not think.
Just draw.*

Letters to the Forgotten
Your Struggles Do Not Define You

Letters to the Forgotten
Your Struggles Do Not Define You

CHAPTER TEN

A Letter To Those Searching For Self-Love:
You Already Have It

You feel sad.
You visit a psychologist.
She spends an hour explaining what you already know.

You leave.
Feeling unfulfilled.
Still sad.

Letters to the Forgotten
Your Struggles Do Not Define You

You visit a psychiatrist.
He writes up a prescription in a blink of an eye and sends you on your way.

You take the drug.
Wait 3 days.
Still sad.
But now with an empty wallet.

You sit on the curb.
Confused.
Drugs in one hand.
Knife in the other.
You are tired of being your own worst enemy.

You want it to stop.
You do your research.
20 self-help books.
30 self-love blogs.
Nothing.

You still feel sad.
You lie in bed, unable to sleep, wondering why you even exist.
You stay silent.
Tears drip down your cheeks.
Silence.
Quiet.

But then you hear something.

Letters to the Forgotten
Your Struggles Do Not Define You

A brisk and mellow gust of wind.
It goes away.
Silence.
Quiet.

You hear it again.
A brisk and mellow gust of wind.
It goes away.
Silence.
Quiet.

You find it strange.
Why is this wind coming and going, intermittently?
Windows are shut.
Doors are closed.

You realize what it is.
Breath.
You are breathing.
You don't ever notice it, but you are breathing.
You spend all this time wondering why you struggle to love yourself.

But you already do.
If you didn't, you would not still be alive.
If you did not have self-love and self-care, you would not be breathing.

You already have self-love.

Letters to the Forgotten
Your Struggles Do Not Define You

You already know what your mind and your body needs, even without the help of anyone else.
Your body is intrinsically capable of self-care.
It is your mind that you let become polluted by the toxicity and chaos around you.

You are told that you must achieve self-love the same way as everyone else.
You are told that you must climb a specific ladder into transcendence.
But you don't have to.
You are already there.

Letters to the Forgotten
Your Struggles Do Not Define You

Write down all the words that are running
Through your head this very moment.
Do not think.
Just write.

Letters to the Forgotten
Your Struggles Do Not Define You

Draw an image that represents how
you are feeling this very moment.
Do not think.
Just draw.

Letters to the Forgotten
Your Struggles Do Not Define You

Letters to the Forgotten
Your Struggles Do Not Define You

LETTERS TO ME

Letters to the Forgotten
Your Struggles Do Not Define You

As part of your own self-love journey, here are some prompts to write your own letters of hope, what you wish to accomplish and feel, how you dream to move on from this dread you are currently facing, and channel the inner strength you have to empower yourself.

Letters to the Forgotten
Your Struggles Do Not Define You

Letters to the Forgotten
Your Struggles Do Not Define You

A Letter To Those Fighting To Survive: Live, So Others Can Also Live

Letters to the Forgotten
Your Struggles Do Not Define You

Letters to the Forgotten
Your Struggles Do Not Define You

A Letter To Those Who Struggle To Forgive Themselves: Seek Forgiveness From Those Who Believe You Deserve Forgiveness

Letters to the Forgotten
Your Struggles Do Not Define You

Letters to the Forgotten
Your Struggles Do Not Define You

A Letter To Those Who Have Been Rejected:
Those Who Rejected You Only Deprived Themselves

Letters to the Forgotten
Your Struggles Do Not Define You

Letters to the Forgotten
Your Struggles Do Not Define You

A Letter To Those Who Do Not Believe In Themselves: Live For Today, And Eventually You Will

Letters to the Forgotten
Your Struggles Do Not Define You

Letters to the Forgotten
Your Struggles Do Not Define You

A Letter To Those Who Find It Difficult To Speak Up:
Be The Courageous Ones Who Stand Up For Those Who Cannot

Letters to the Forgotten
Your Struggles Do Not Define You

Letters to the Forgotten
Your Struggles Do Not Define You

A Letter To Those Who Need A Supportive Hand: I Am Here, And I Am Not Going Anywhere

Letters to the Forgotten
Your Struggles Do Not Define You

EPILOGUE

Reminder To Love Everyone

The ones who hold the biggest smiles are not always the ones who are happiest.
The ones who yell out the biggest cries are not always the ones in need of help.
The ones who seem to have it all together are not always the most successful.

Letters to the Forgotten
Your Struggles Do Not Define You

The ones who say the most words are not always the most intelligent.
The ones with the most hope are not always the most courageous.
The last souls standing are not always the strongest.

Everyone has their own struggles, their own strengths, and their own demons.
Just because someone seems like they are fine, does not necessarily mean that they are.

Just because someone is not outwardly struggling as much as others, does not mean that they are not struggling internally. We never know how our words and our actions affect others because the faces they show on the outside are not always the ones they feel on the inside.

We all have darkness in our corners, and we all have faces and secrets that we hide from others.
If the person next to you seems happier than you do, do not assume that they are not sad.
If the person next to you seems miserable, do not assume that they do not have hope and a fighting chance at life.

Be the person who learns to read people by interacting with them and learning about who they really are rather than predicting how they are based on their appearances.

Letters to the Forgotten
Your Struggles Do Not Define You

Your happy-go-lucky neighbor can very well be struggling with depression while you are too busy focusing on those crying for help.

Do not assume.
Listen.
Open your heart to everyone.

Letters to the Forgotten
Your Struggles Do Not Define You

Letters to the Forgotten
Your Struggles Do Not Define You

www.ingramcontent.com/pod-product-compliance
Lightning Source LLC
Chambersburg PA
CBHW052106070526
44584CB00017B/2358